JOHN DENVER

GREATEST HITS
Volume 3

Francois Lehr/SIPA Press

Contents

Edited by Milton Okun

Art Director: Dan Recchia

ISBN: 0-89524-294-X

HOW CAN I LEAVE YOU AGAIN

Words and Music by John Denver

Chorus

8

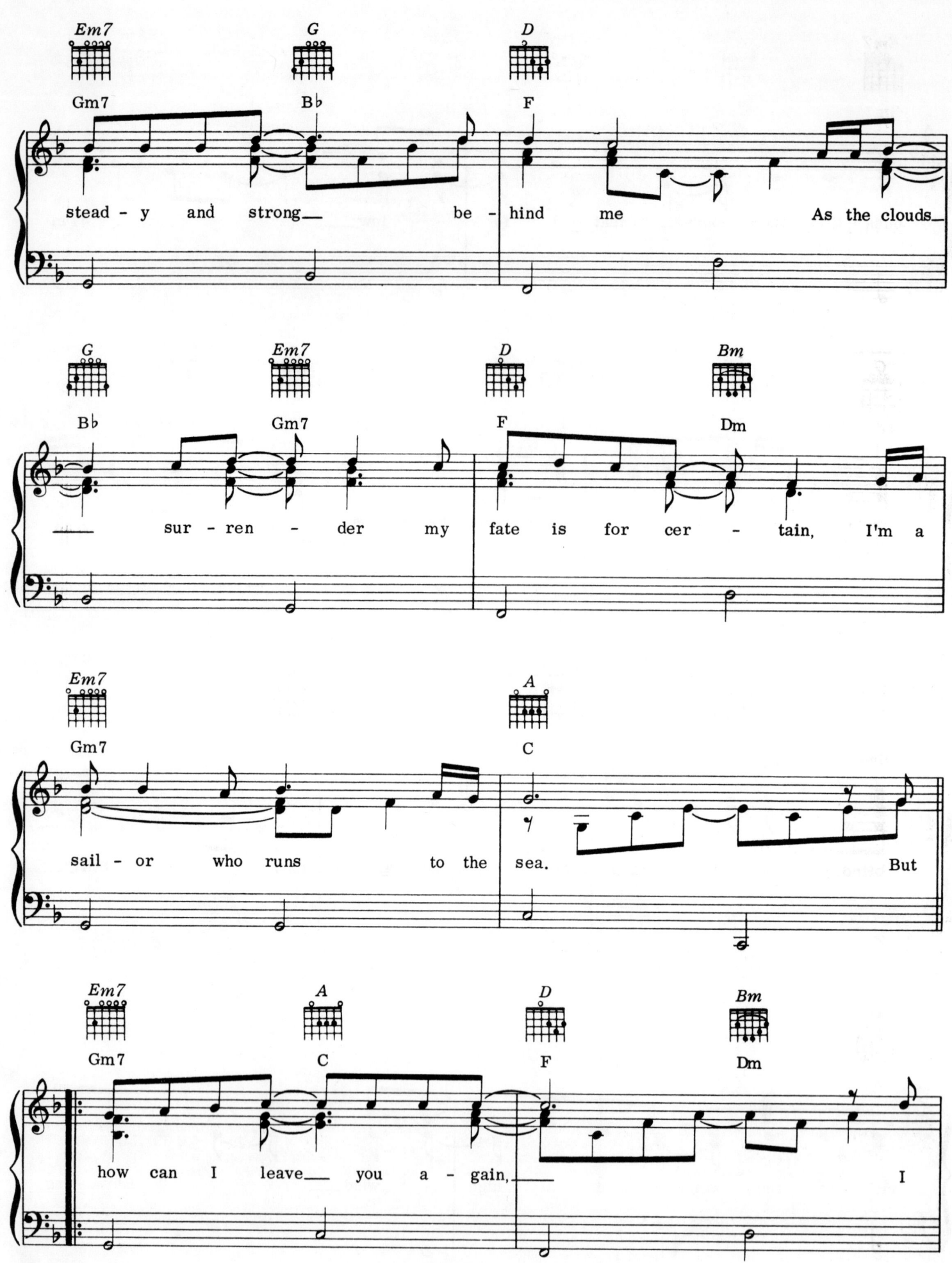

must be clear out of my mind,___ Lost in a storm_ I've gone

1. blind,_____ Oh, how can I leave you a-gain.___

2. blind,___ Oh, how___ can I leave you a-gain.

SOME DAYS ARE DIAMONDS
(Some Days Are Stone)

Words and Music by Dick Feller

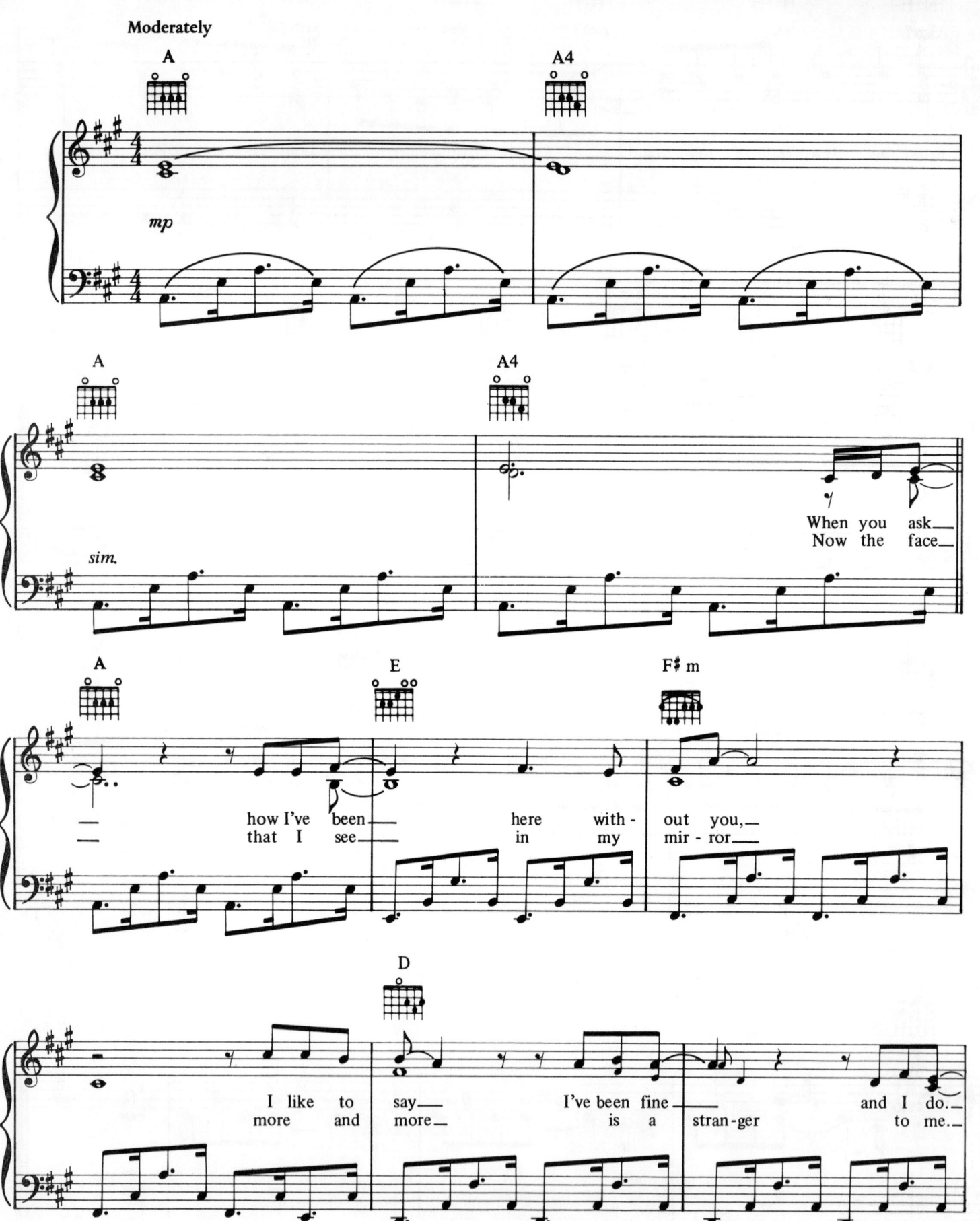

16

SHANGHAI BREEZES

Slowly

Words and Music by John Denver

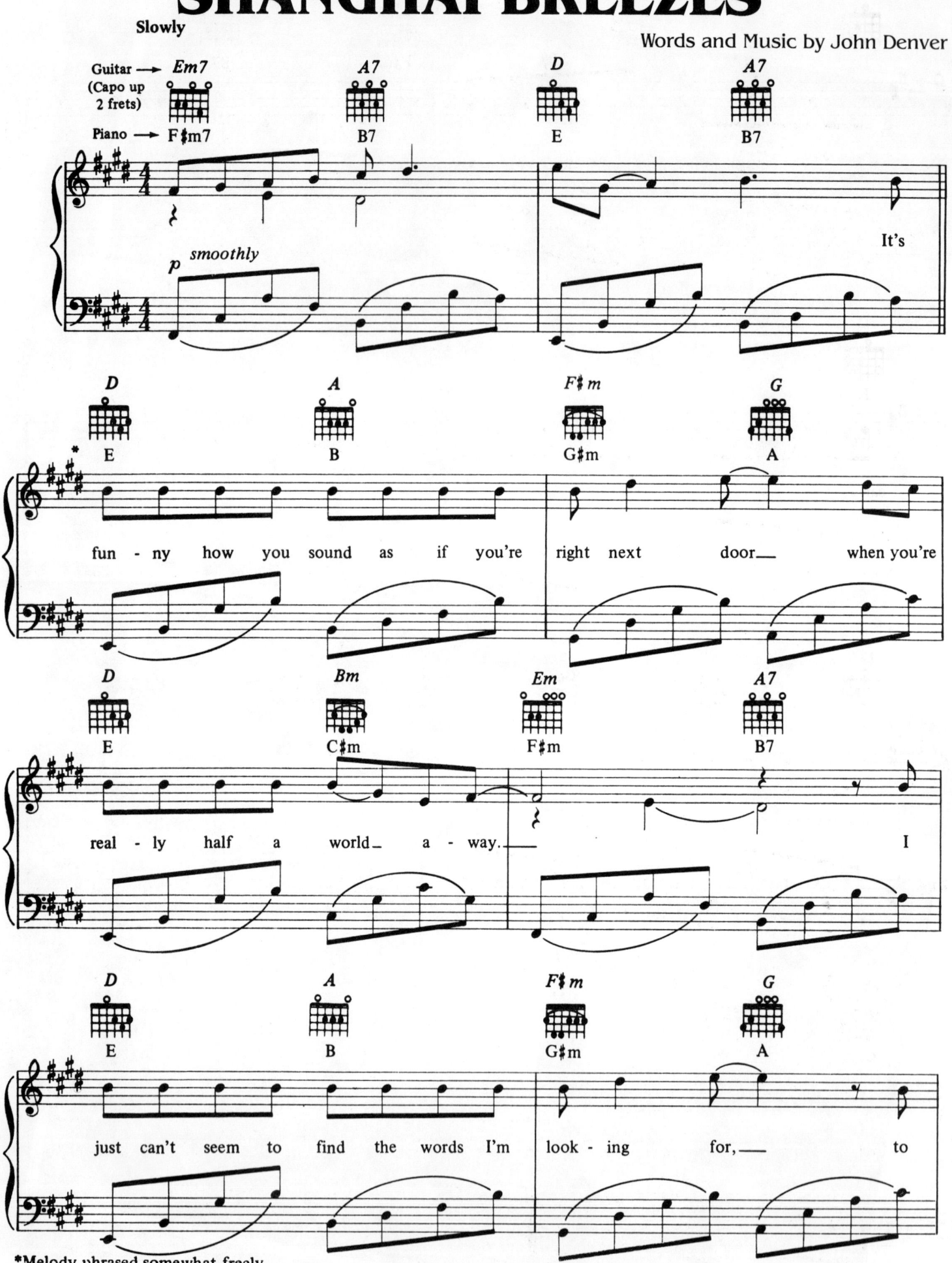

*Melody phrased somewhat freely.

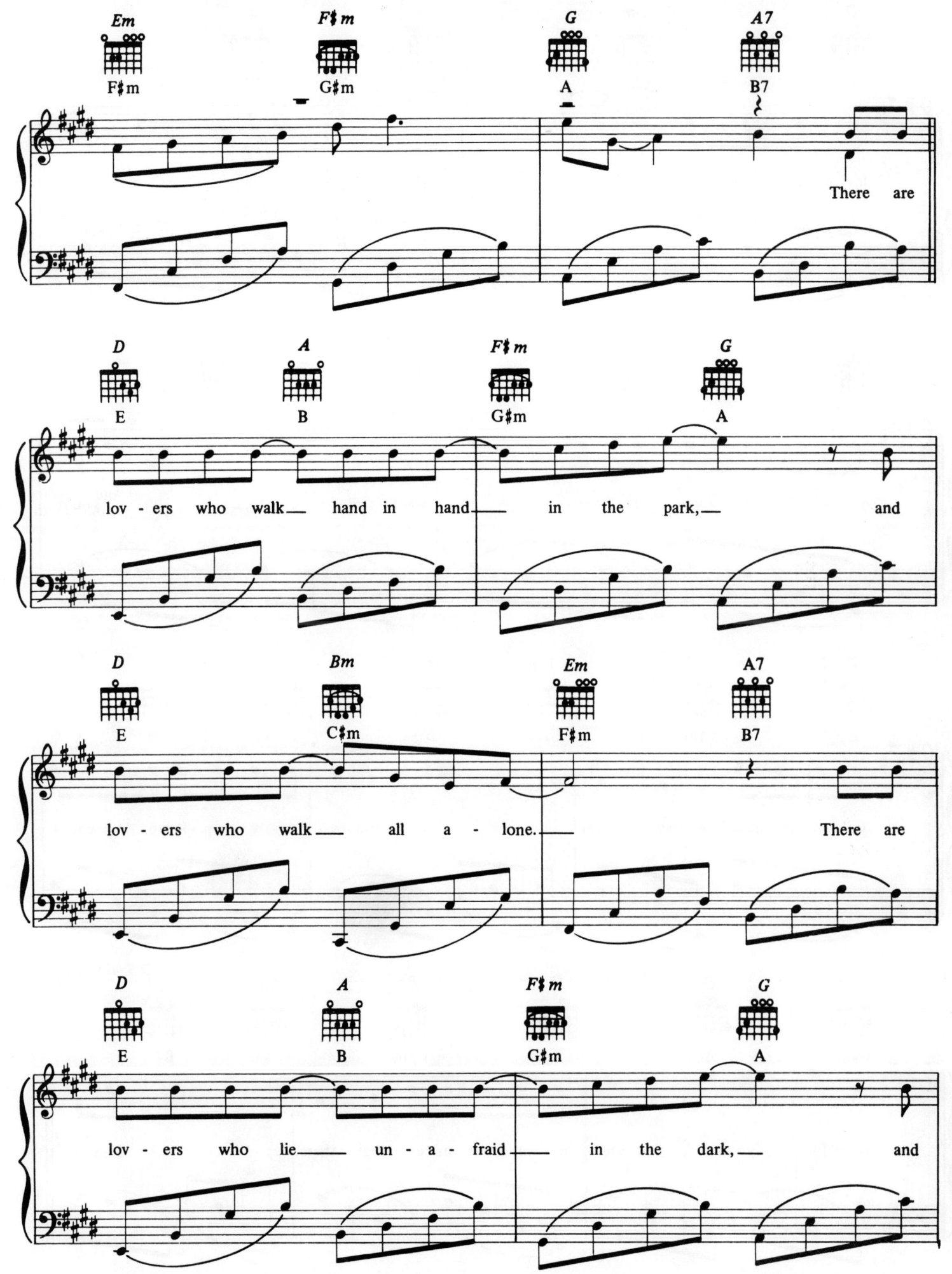

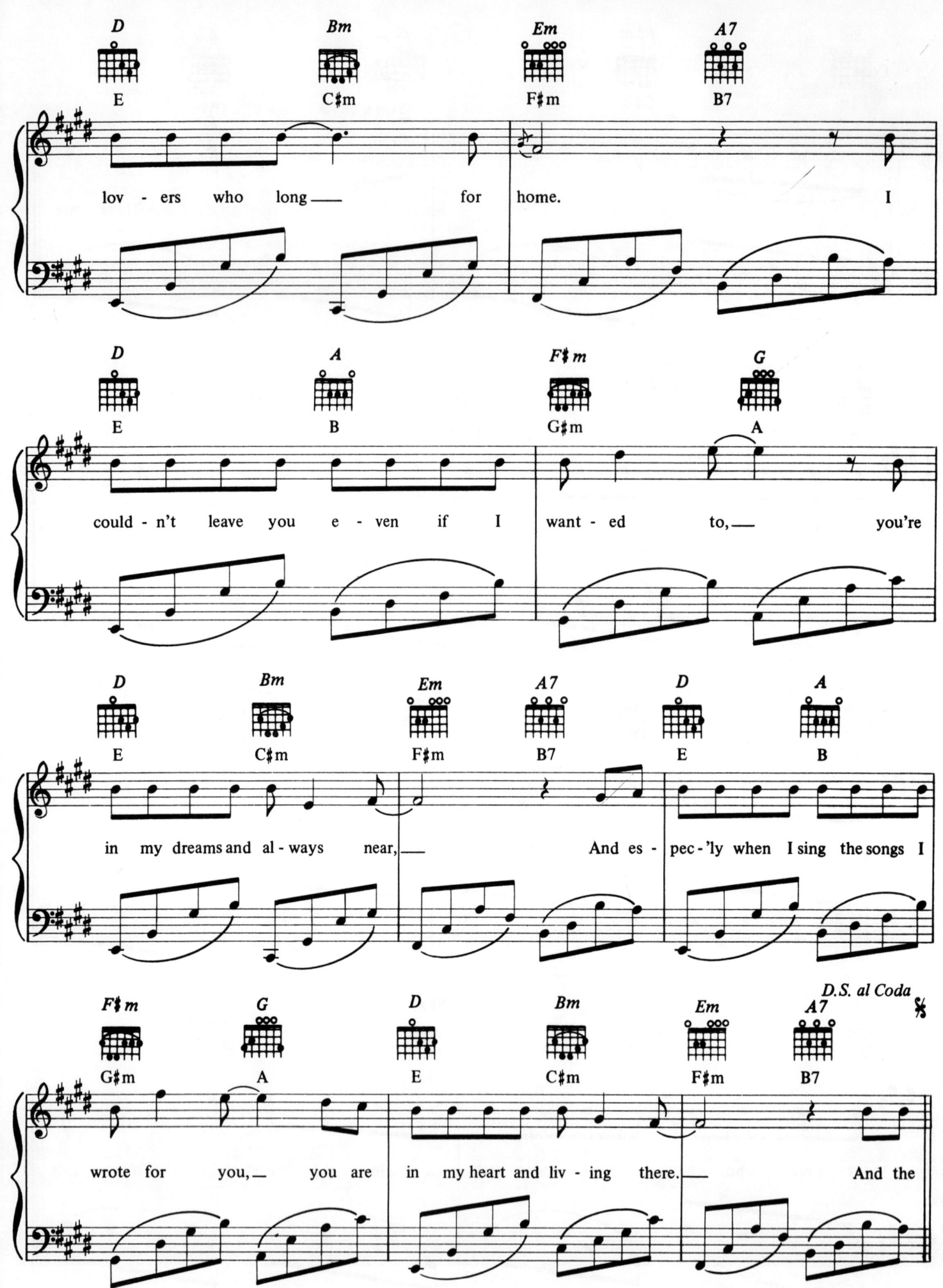

22

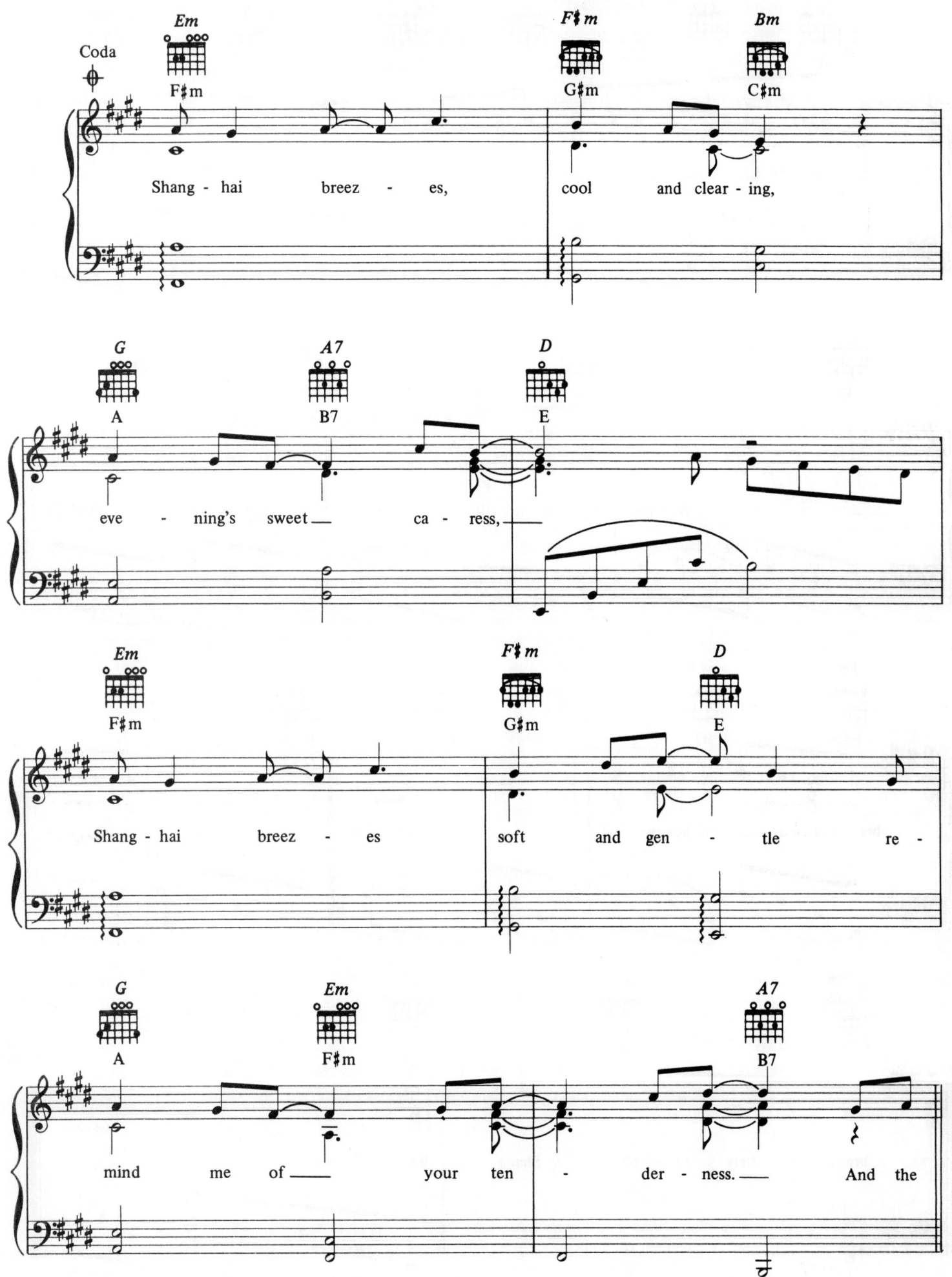

23

moon and the stars— are the same— ones you see,— it's the same old sun up in the sky.

— And your love in my life— is like heav - en to me,— like the

breez - es here in old Shang - hai.— And the Just like the

slightly held back

breez - es here in old Shang - hai.

slower

LOVE AGAIN
As recorded by John Denver and Sylvie Vartan

Words and Music by John Denver

Moderately slow (♩ = 104)

I did-n't think it could hap-pen a-gain, I'm just too old and set in my ways. I was con-vinced I would al-ways be lone-ly all of the rest of my days. May-be I gave up on ro-mance in my

long-ing to give up the pain; I just did-n't be-lieve I would ev-

er love a-gain.

I was like one who had shut my-self in, closed the win-dows, locked all the doors
What does it take for a blind man to see that there's more there than just meets the eye?

A-fraid of the dark and the beat of my heart, and yet
What are the ways that the mag-ic comes in, that can

may-be it's_ just_ that I'm fall - ing in love_ a - gain._ (Or may - be it's just_ that I'm

fall - ing in love_ a - gain.) _ *(For guitar duet arrangement of this solo, see page   )*

SEASONS OF THE HEART

Slowly

Words and Music by John Denver

31

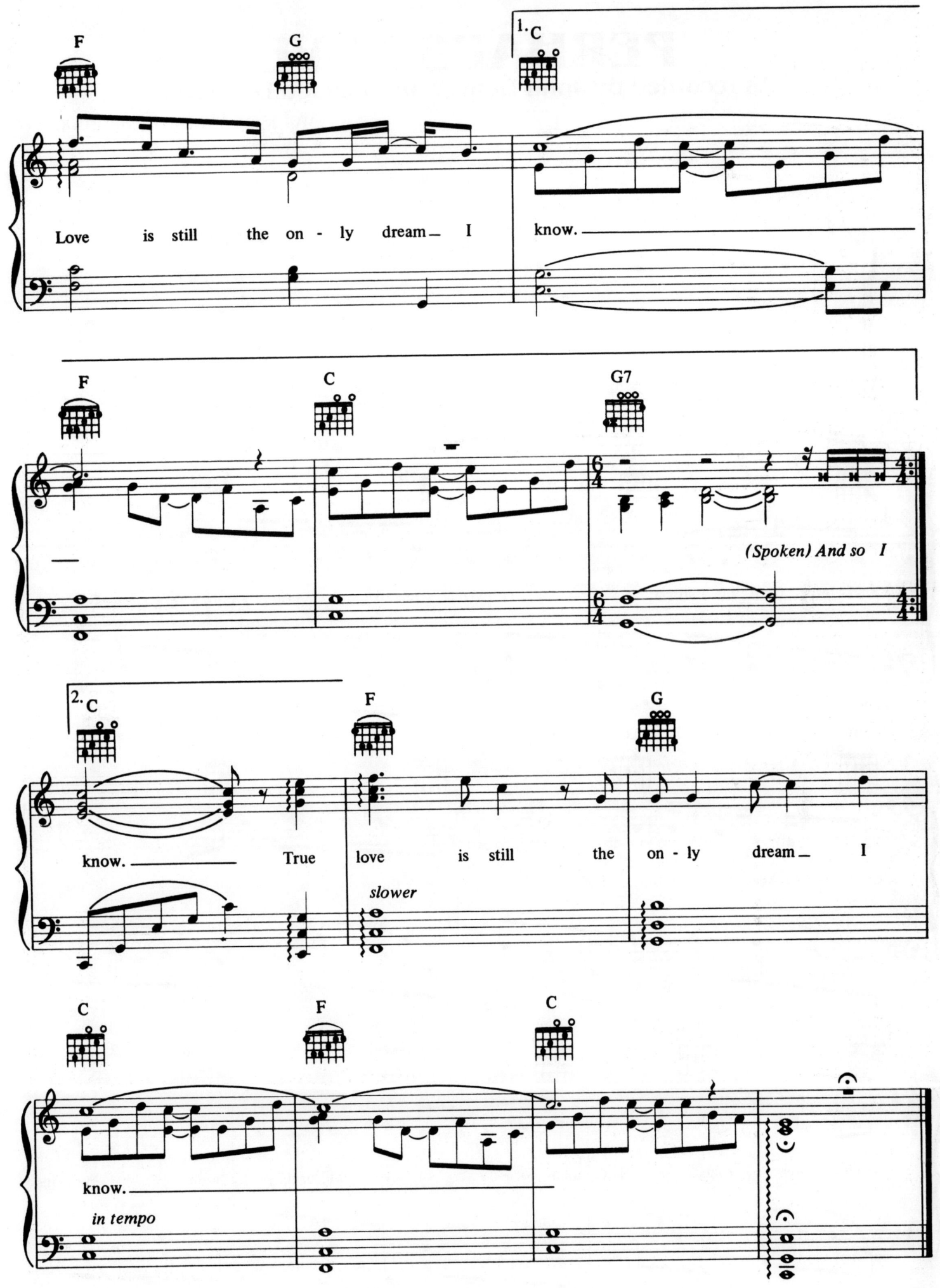

PERHAPS LOVE
As recorded by John Denver and Placido Domingo

Words and Music by John Denver

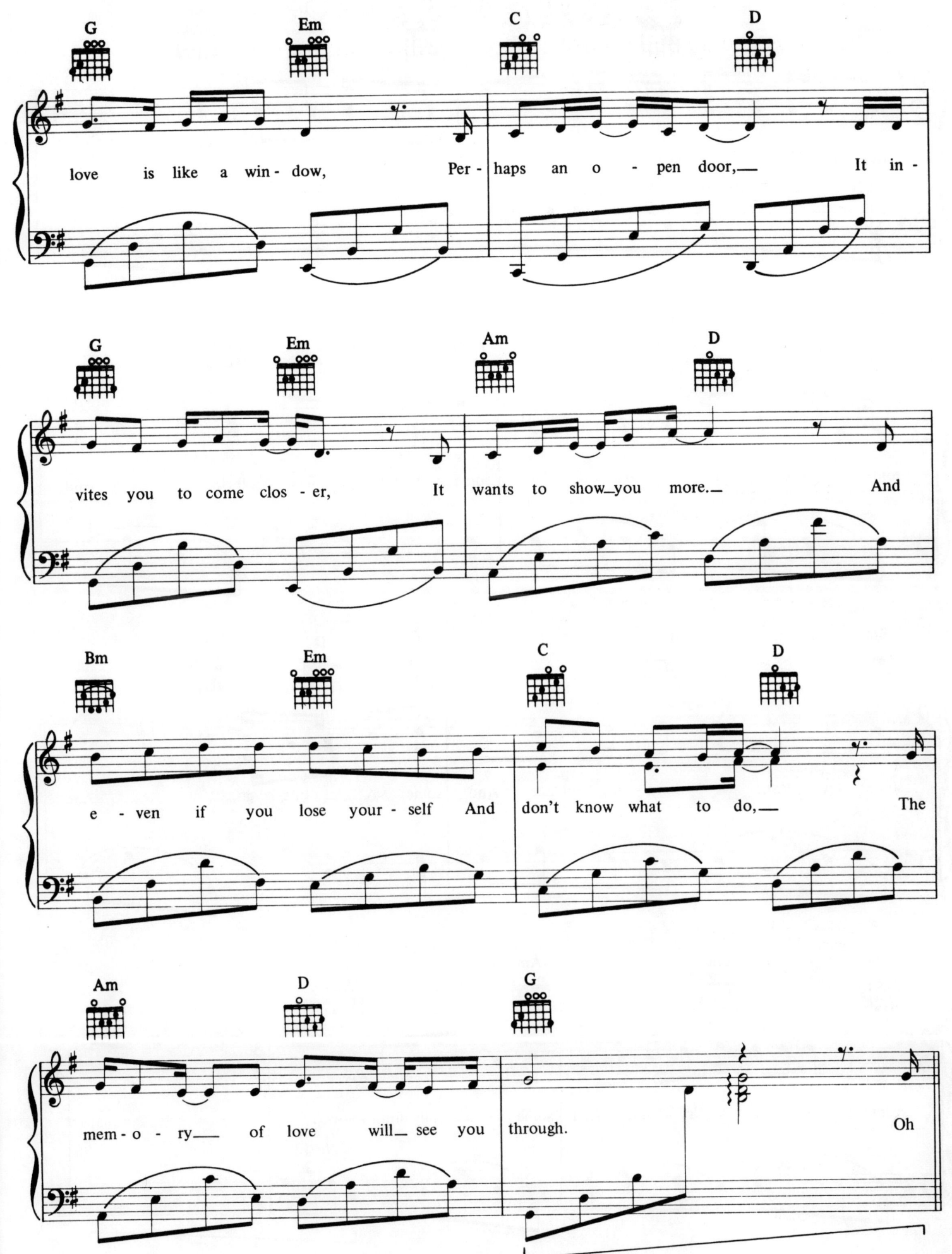

love to some___ is like a cloud,___ to some as___ strong___ as steel, For

some a way___ of liv - ing, For some a way___ to feel, And

some say love is hold - ing on,___ And some say let - ting go,___ And

some say love_ is ev - 'ry - thing,_ And some say___ they don't know... Per - haps

slightly   held back

love is like the o-cean, Full of con-flict, full of change, Like a

in tempo

fire___ when it's cold_out-side,___ Or thun-der when it rains.___ If

I should live for-ev-er And all my dreams come true, My

mem-o-ries___ of love will_ be of you.

slowing

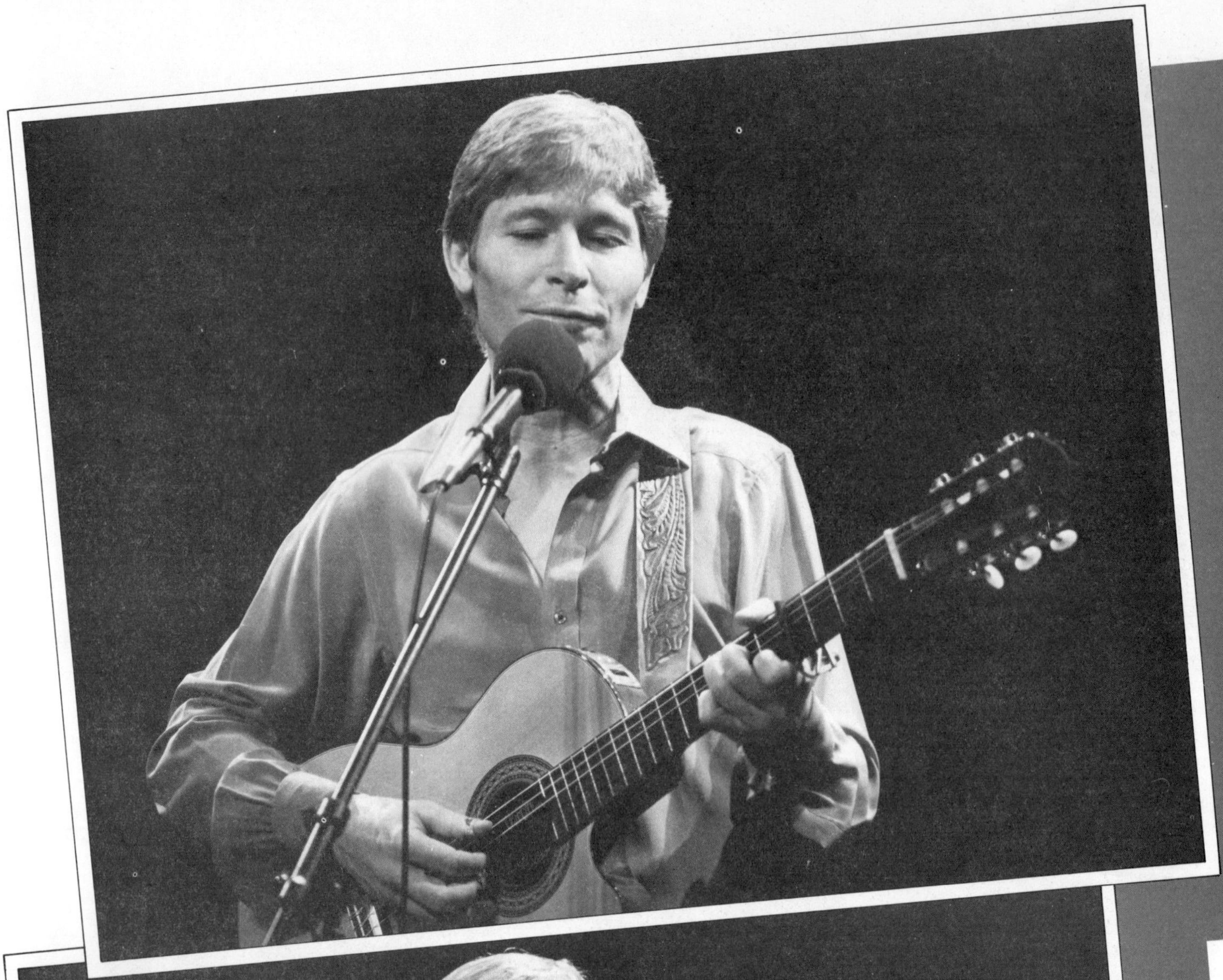
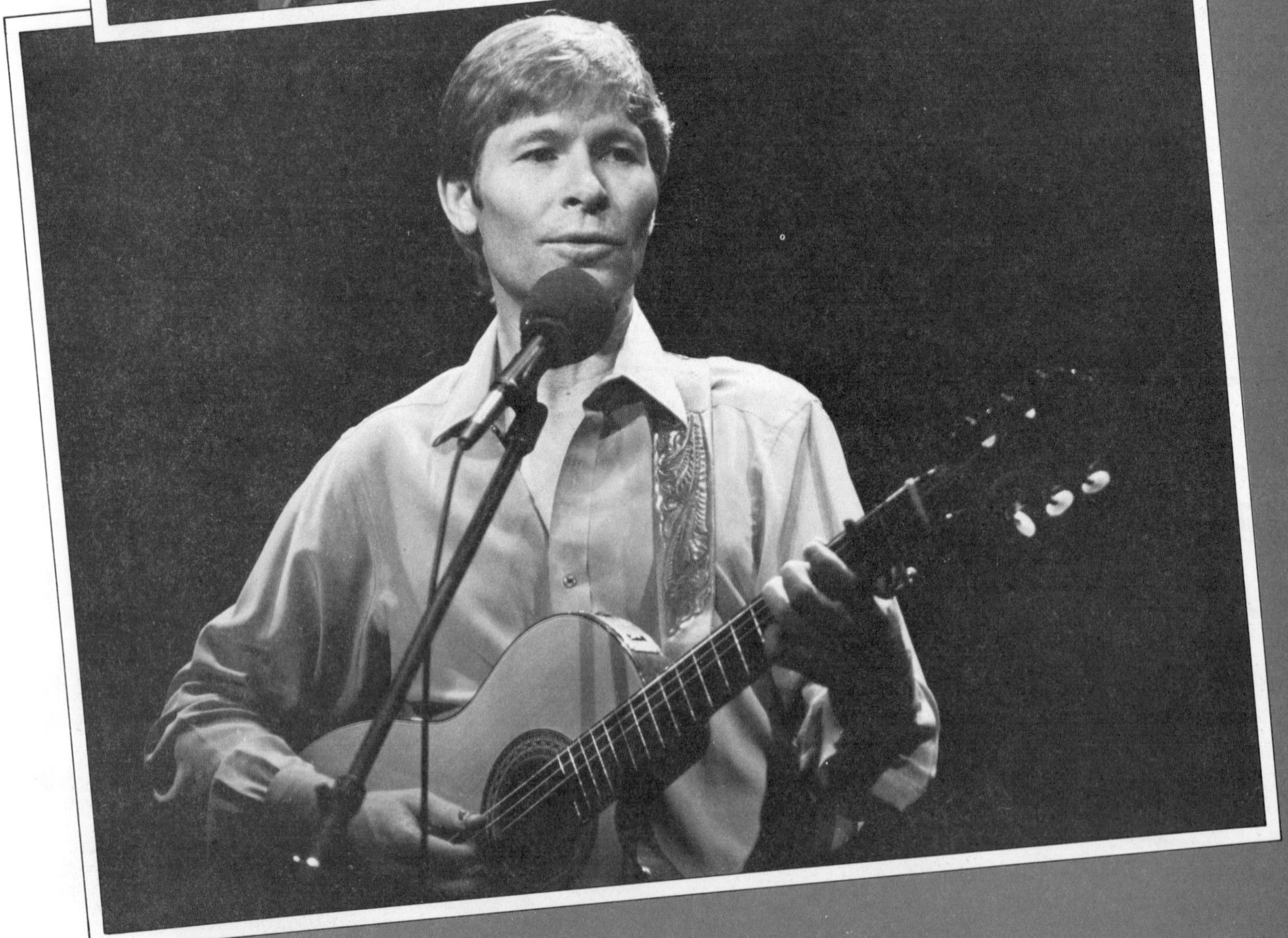

DANCING WITH THE MOUNTAINS

Words and Music by John Denver

*Guitarists: Tune 6th string to D

stretch your soul.___

Just re - lax___ and let the rhy - thm___ take___ you,
Were you___ there___ the night they lost the___ light - ning?

Don't you___ be___ a - fraid to lose con - trol.___
Were you___ there___ the day the earth stood still?___

If your___ heart___ has found some
Did you___ see___ the fa - mous

emp - ty___ spa - ces,
and the___ fight - ing,

Danc - in's___ just___ a thing to make you whole.___
Did you___ hear___ the pro - phet tell his tale?___

G   D

I   am one   who danc - es with___ the moun -
We   are one,   when danc - ing with___ the moun -

tains; _____
tains,   wo,

*Final fade omitted

WILD MONTANA SKIES
As recorded by John Denver and Emmylou Harris

Words and Music by John Denver

* Guitarists: Tune 6th string to D

mother took him to her breast and softly she did sing: Oh —

Chorus

oh Montana, give this child a home, — Give him the love —

— of a good fam-'ly and a woman of his own — Give him a

fire in his heart, give him a light — in his eyes, — Give him the wild —

wind for a broth - er and the wild_____

_____ Mon - tan - a skies.

His moth - er died that

sum - mer,_____ he nev - er learned to cry,_____ He

never knew his fa - ther, he never did ask why And he never knew the an - swers that would make an eas - y way, But he learned to know the wil - der-ness and to be a man that way. His

On the
Now

eve of his twen-ty first birth-day he set out on his own, He was
some say he was cra-zy some are glad he's gone, But

thir-ty years and run-nin' when he found his way back home Rid-in' a storm
some of us will miss him and we'll try to car-ry on Giv-ing a voice

a-cross the moun-tains and an ach-in' in his heart. Said he
to the for-est, giv-ing a voice. to the dawn, Giv-ing a voice

* 2nd time instrumental omitted

50

in his eyes, Give him the wild ___ wind for a broth - er and the

wild _____ Mon - tan - a skies. _____ Oh ___

wild _____ Mon - tan - a skies. _____

THE GOLD AND BEYOND

As sung at the '84 Winter Olympics

Music by John Denver and Lee Holdridge
Words by John Denver

dream of a life time is won. _____ There's a

fire in the heart and it feels like the hun - ger, _____
eyes of the moun - tain all peo - ple are e - qual, _____

____ The spir - it is burn - ing con - sumed by a
In the eyes of all peo - ple our soul can be

flame; _____ To be one of the best of the
seen; _____ In the course of our strug - gle we'll

all that you can be and all that you've ev - er longed for!

all that you can be and all that you've ev - er longed for!

pianists: omit

(to Coda)

To Coda

D.S. al Coda

dim.

In the

56

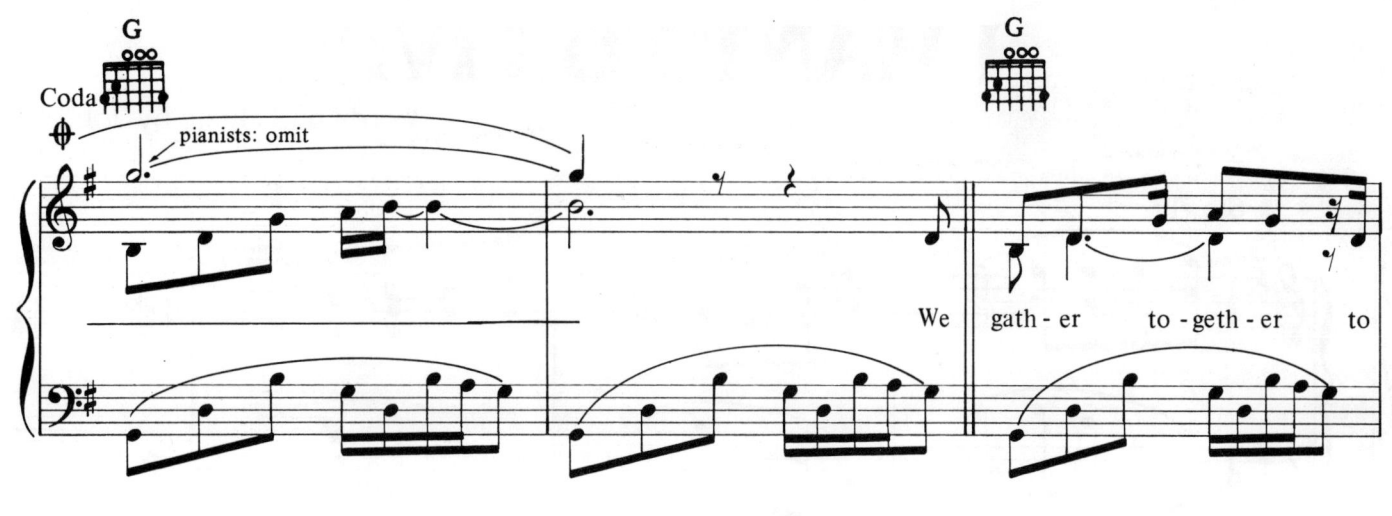

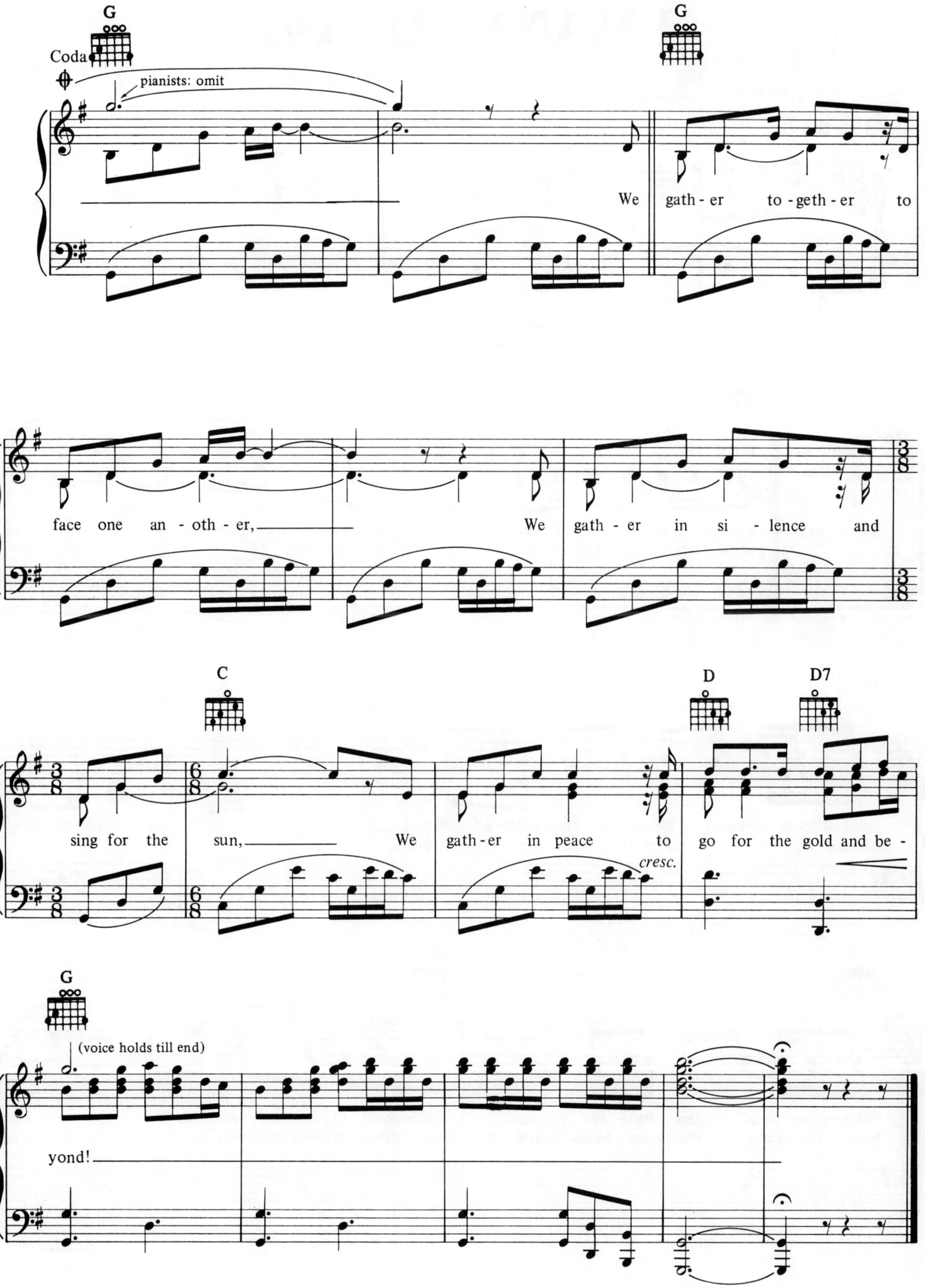
G
Coda
pianists: omit
G
We gath-er to-geth-er to
face one an-oth-er,
We gath-er in si-lence and
sing for the
C
sun,
We gath-er in peace to
cresc.
D
D7
go for the gold and be-
G
(voice holds till end)
yond!

I WANT TO LIVE

Words and Music by John Denver

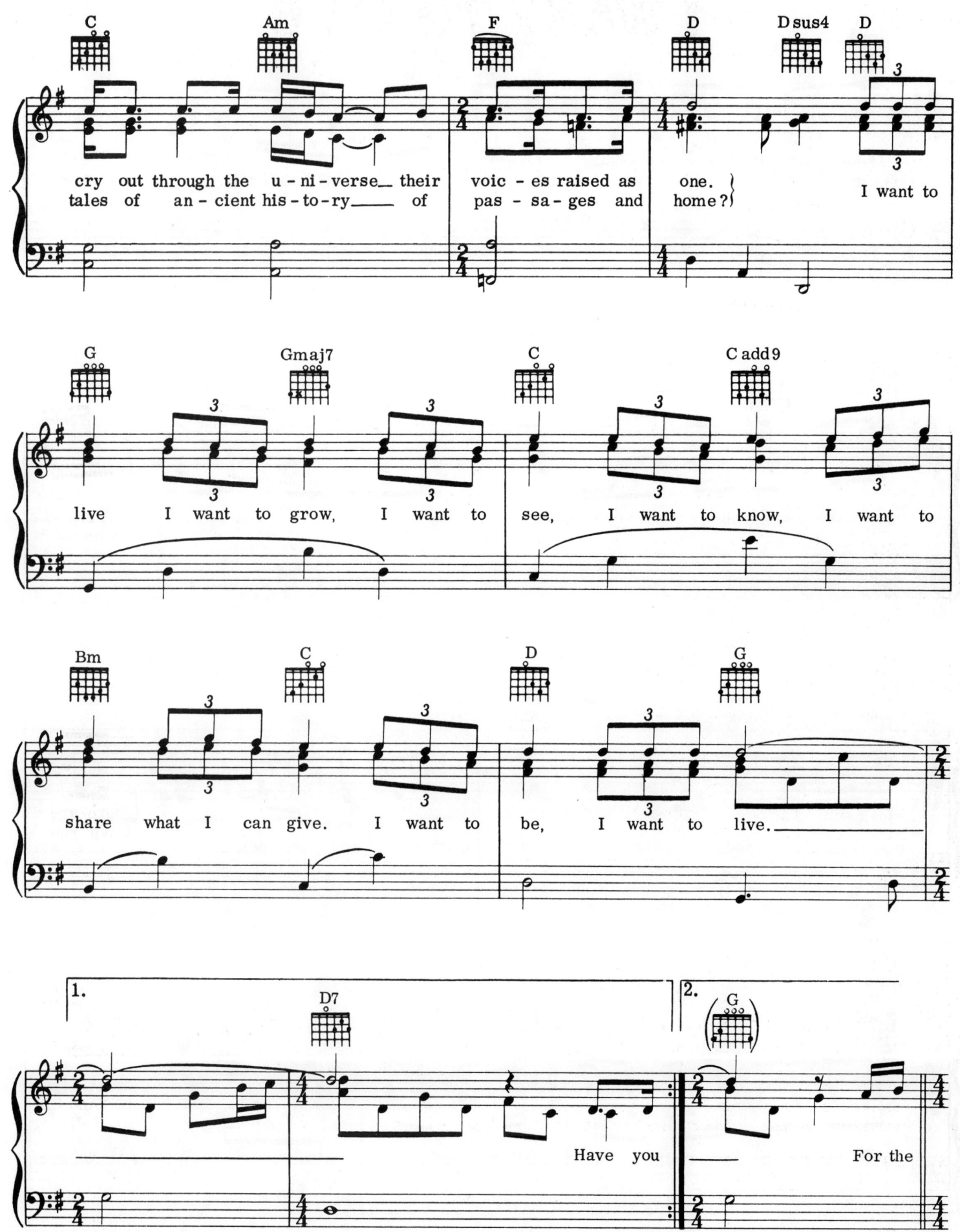

standing all together face to face and arm in arm. We are

standing on the threshold of a dream, No more

hunger, no more killing, no more wasting life away; It is

simply an idea and I know its time has come. I want to

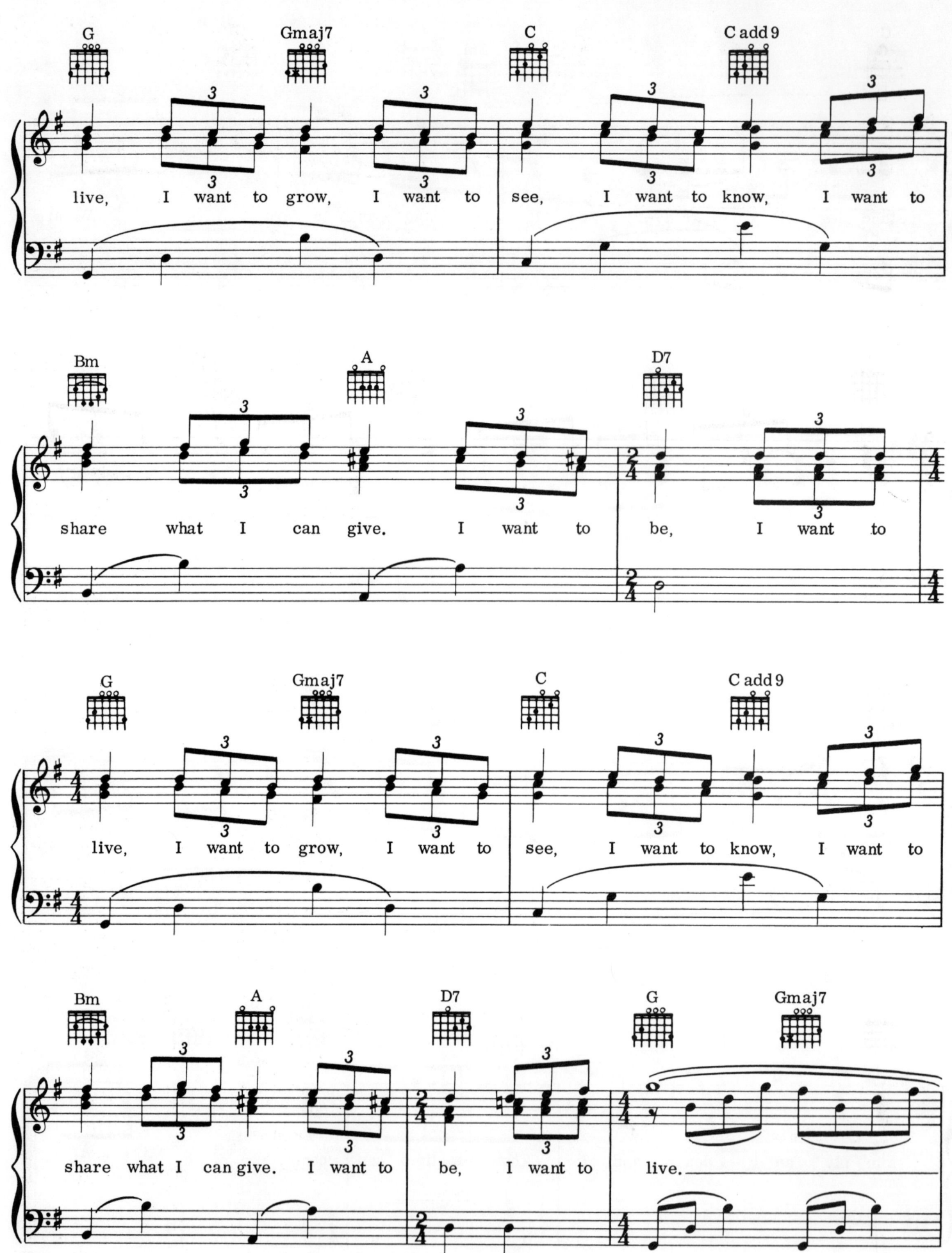

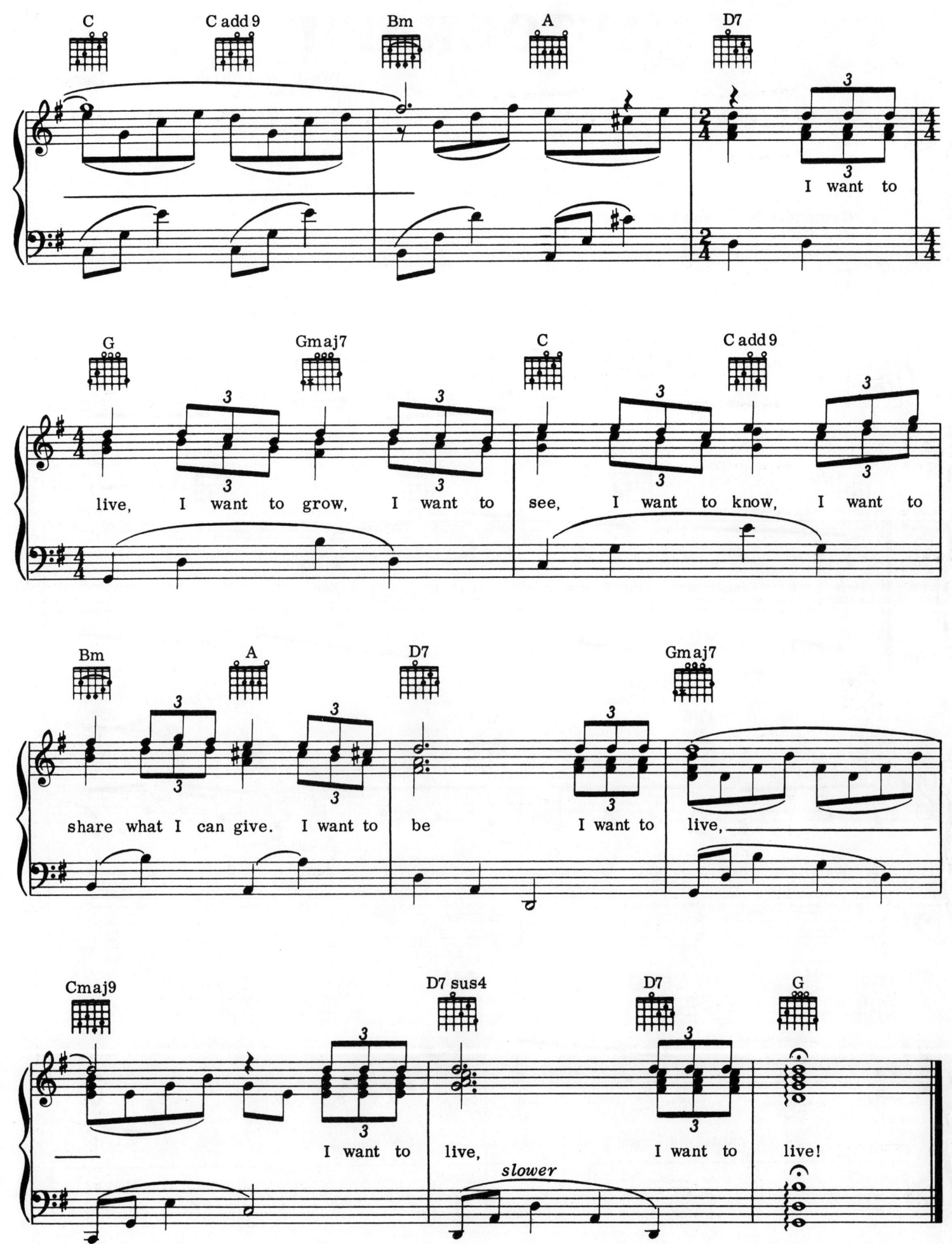

AUTOGRAPH

Words and Music by John Denver

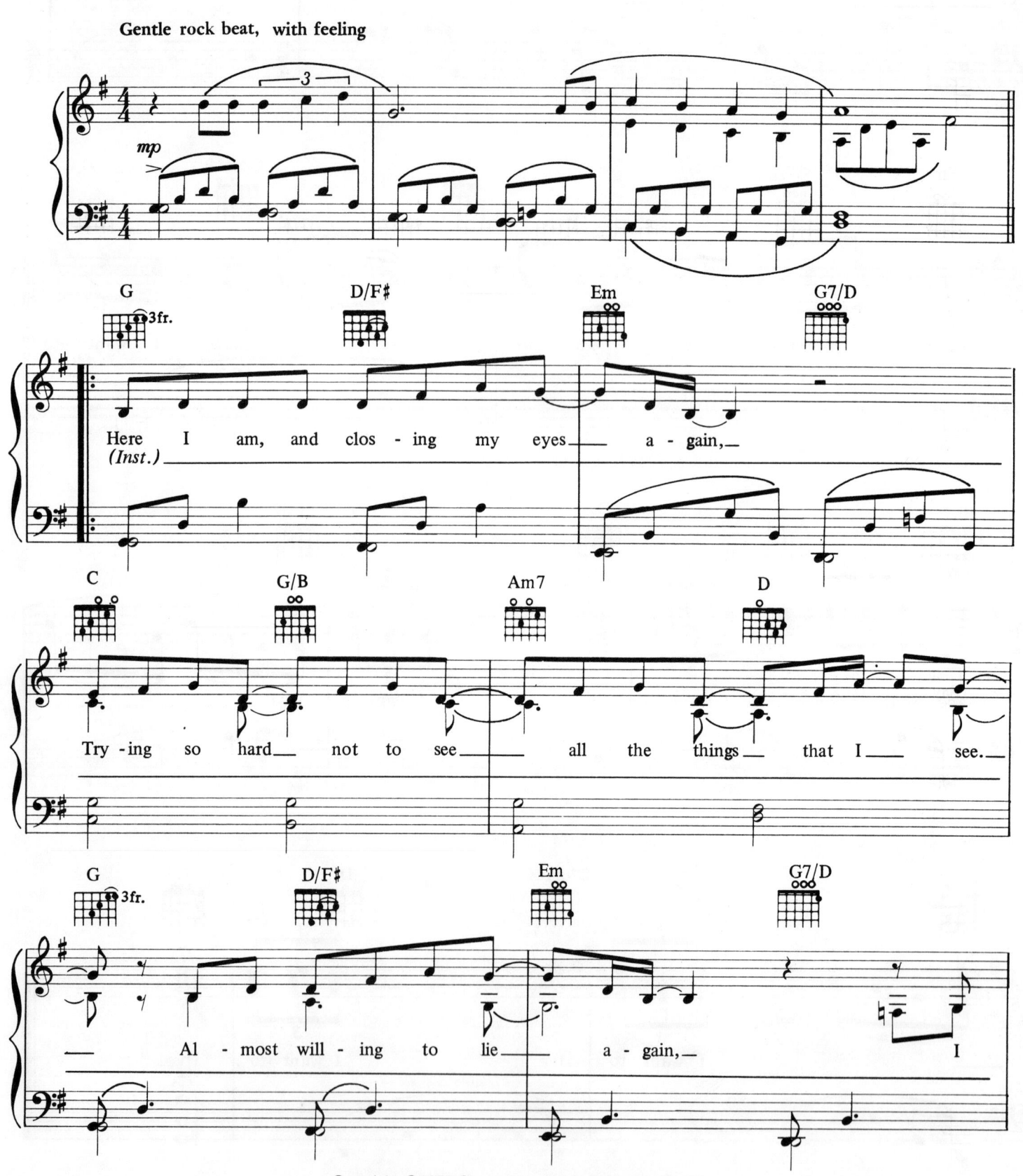

JOHN DENVER

Aerie

All the songs from the album, including *Friends With You, Casey's Last Ride, The Eagle And The Hawk.*
#9007 $4.95

An Evening With John Denver

All 23 songs from the popular double album, including *Annie's Song, Grandma's Feather Bed, Sweet Surrender, Rocky Mountain High,* plus color photos.
#9002 $9.95

Farewell Andromeda

All the songs from the album and more from John's T.V. Special *Big Horn; I'd Rather Be A Cowboy, Rocky Mountain Suite, Angels From Montgomery,* plus color photos.
9006 $6.95

JD John Denver

Matching folio includes *Sweet Melinda, You're So Beautiful, Johnny B. Goode.* 11 Songs in all plus full color photos.
#9013 $6.95

John Denver Anthology Piano Vocal

A superb volume of over 80 of Denver's best-loved songs; *Rocky Mountain High, Sunshine On My Shoulders, Annie's Song, Country Love, Take Me Home, Country Roads.* Features biography, photos and John Denver's thoughts behind many of the songs.
9017 $17.95

John Denver's Greatest Hits-Vol. 1

Matching folio to smash LP contains *Sunshine On My Shoulders, Take Me Home, Country Roads, Follow Me,* plus photos and lyric sheets.
#9010 $8.95

John Denver's Greatest Hits.-Vol.2

Matching folio to the gold album features *Annie's Song, Fly Away, Calypso, I'm Sorry, Back Home Again, Welcome To My Morning.*
#9011 $8.95

John Denver Greatest Hits-Vol. 3

Matching folio includes the hits *Shanghai Breezes, Perhaps Love,* and *Some Days Are Diamonds,* plus the giant country hit *Wild Montana Skies,* and Denver's song for the 1984 Winter Olympics, *The Gold And Beyond.*
#9021 $9.95

The John Denver Songbook

Deluxe selection from John's first four best selling albums; *Take Me Home, Country Roads. Poems, Prayers And Promises, My Sweet Lady,* plus photos, woodprints and autobiographical notes.
#9003 $9.95

Rocky Mountain High

Matching folio to the album containing *Goodbye Again, For Baby (For Bobbie), The Season Suite* and *Rocky Mountain High.*
#9005 $6.95

Seasons Of The Heart

Matching folio to John Denver's album. 4-color photos plus 11 songs, including his hits *Perhaps Love* and *Shanghai Breezes.*
9018 $9.95

Some Days Are Diamonds

Matching folio contains 10 arrangements, including the title tune *Some Days Are Diamonds, The Cowboy And The Lady, Country Love,* plus photos and lyric section.
#9016 $6.95

Spirit

Matching the hit LP, folio contains *Like A Sad Song, Wrangell Mountain Song, It Makes Me Giggle,* plus full color photos.
#9008 $6.95

Windsong

Full color photos and lyric sheets enchance this matching folio to the gold album. Songs include *Calypso, Windsong, Fly Away, Looking For Space* and *I'm Sorry.*
#9001 $6.95

AVAILABLE NOW AT YOUR LOCAL MUSIC DEALER

Cherry Lane Music Co., inc.
"quality in printed music"
P.O. BOX 430 • PORT CHESTER, NY 10573